Sing
Praises
to His
Name

Sing Praises to His Name

WORSHIP RESOURCES
FOR THE CHRISTIAN CONGREGATION

LOUIS PRATT

C.S.S. Publishing Co., Inc.
Lima, Ohio

SING PRAISES TO HIS NAME

Copyright © 1986 by
The C.S.S. Publishing Company, Inc.
Lima, Ohio

6845 / ISBN 0-89536-831-5

PRINTED IN U.S.A.

Table of Contents

Introduction 7

Calls to Worship 11

Prayers of Confession 31

Prayers of Celebration 67

General Prayers 77

Introduction

In his book *Reality In Worship* Willard L. Sperry wrote:

> . . . there remains to the church one unique and peculiar responsibility
> . . . the conduct of public worship . . . If the church does nothing other
> than to keep open a house symbolic of the homeland of the soul where
> in season and out, women and men come to reenact the memory and
> vision of who they are, it will have rendered society and each
> of us, a service of unmeasureable value.

These words are as true today as they were when Dean Sperry wrote them many years ago. Worship is the central enduring act shared by Christian people.

There is always need for resources with which public worship can be enriched. In this volume, *Sing Praises To His Name,* Louis Pratt provides such resources. Consisting of calls to worship, prayers of confession, prayers of celebration, general prayers, this book will long serve persons who turn to it in the quest for useable worship resources.

Louis Pratt is a thoughtful, sensitive pastor. The writings in this book reflect the spirit of devotion, together with insight into the struggles and joys of the Christian life. While the materials have been intended primarily for use in public worship, many individuals will find rich resources here in their private devotions.

Harvey Potthoff
Professor Emeritus,
Iliff School of Theology

Part 1

Calls to Worship

1

Leader: Wait on the Lord, for he will not desert you. Stand, and do not fear the forces which stand against you.

People: But life seems so overwhelming at times, and we seem so alone.

Leader: We are never alone, for God is always with us. Hold firm to your faith, and God will sustain you.

People: Come, Lord, console our hearts and strengthen our resolve.

2

Leader: Come to the Lord, whose name is love, and you will find peace in your heart.

People: Thank you, Lord, for loving us when we were so unlovable.

Leader: Take up your cross of love and follow the Lord.

People: We will do our best, Lord, to follow you in a way that gives credit to you.

3

Leader: Worship the Lord and contemplate his majesty.

People: Praise the Lord, for his greatness exceeds our understanding.

Leader: Serve the Lord with gladness, for in serving him we find life.

People: We offer ourselves, Lord, as instruments for your love and righteousness.

4

Leader: With what should we come before the Lord?

People: With lives dedicated to his service.

Leader: Let us, then, attune our hearts and minds so that we may better learn what he would have us do.

People: Enter our hearts, Lord; speak to us in the silence of our hearts as we contemplate your message to us today.

Calls to Worship

5

Leader: Seek the Lord, while he may be found, or you may find yourself forever lost.
People: We come, Lord, seeking your presence in our lives.
Leader: Serve the Lord with a heart full of devotion.
People: Direct our lives in the way you would have us go, Lord. We will do our best to follow Christ.

6

Leader: What are you doing here?
People: We have come to worship God, and to thank him for his many blessings.
Leader: Good. God deserves such praise. And are you trying to be forgiving of your enemies, as God demands of us?
People: Yes. And we pray that God will aid us as we pursue the difficult path of forgiveness.
Leader: God will indeed dwell in the hearts of those who pursue the way of forgiveness.
People: Amen.

7

Leader: Let us worship God in gratitude for all that he has done for us.
People: Amen. God has greatly enriched our lives.
Leader: But let us be careful that we not let envy of our neighbors and their gifts undermine our worship.
People: Help us, Lord, to curb all thoughts of resentment and share in the joy of our neighbors over their gifts.

8

Leader: Come and receive the new life Christ has promised.
People: We gladly accept the gift so freely given.
Leader: With thankfulness in our hearts, let us face the coming days.
People: With Christ as our guide and strength, we can face anything.

9

Leader: Let us thank the Lord for his steadfast love, for his wonderful works to all people.

People: **The Lord is good to all, and his compassion is over all that he has made.**

Leader: Blessed be the Lord, our God, who does wondrous things.

People: **Blessed be his glorious name forever; may his glory fill the whole earth!**

10

Leader: Serve the Lord with gladness, and do not presume that past service makes present service unnecessary.

People: **We gladly go when God calls, for in him we find life.**

Leader: True life is this — to work in his vineyard, proclaiming his peace.

People: **We would be your compassionate children, Lord, so others may see your love in us.**

11

Leader: Open now your hearts to God.

People: **We open our hearts and our lives to your presence, Lord. Create in us a clean heart.**

Leader: Let us dedicate our lives to his Gospel.

People: **We dedicate our lives and our possessions to our task of proclaiming the love of God to our love-starved world.**

12

Leader: Know that the Lord is God and that it is he who created us.

People: **Let us praise the Lord for his mighty works.**

Leader: Know that the Lord has called us and has given us a mission.

People: **Let us go forward proclaiming the good news of his love and laboring for the advancement of his kingdom.**

Leader: Be prepared to witness to the hope that is in you.

Calls to Worship

People: **We shall endure, for God is on our side.**

13

Leader: Do not trust in deceptive words: "God is on our side."
Rather, strive to be on God's side.
People: **We put our trust in God and look to him for direction for
our lives.**
Leader: Be not puffed up with pride. Rather, in all humility,
study how you may improve yourselves.
People: **We lay aside all thoughts of pride and seek to fulfill God's
covenant of righteousness.**

14

Leader: Serve the Lord with gladness.
People: **We are here, Lord; command, and we will obey.**
Leader: Discipline your hearts so that you do not fail to be
God's holy and loving people.
People: **With all due respect, Lord, we'd rather not have to work
too hard at it.**
Leader: The way that leads to destruction is easy, but the way
to life makes many demands.
People: **We hear, O Lord, and we obey.**

15

Leader: Come to the Lord, whose love lifts us above all ad-
versity.
People: **Help us, Lord, for our problems often seem about to over-
whelm us.**
Leader: Know that the Lord is God, and he is able to deliver
all those who turn their lives over to him safely into
his presence.
People: **Thank you, Lord, for the love that bring faith and hope into
our lives.**

16

Leader: Christ has come. Let us worship him.

People: With his coming we are healed. Through him we are at one in the Spirit.

Leader: Let us offer him true worship, voices and lives in harmony with his will.

People: He has made us whole. For our sake he died. For his sake we live.

17

Leader: Serve the Lord with a right spirit.

People: What is the right spirit in serving God?

Leader: A spirit of loving service to others, which seeks not your glory but their benefit.

People: We will give of ourselves in service to God and to his people.

18

Leader: Prepare to meet your Lord, for he will come at an hour when you least expect him.

People: We will do our best to be a people prepared for his coming.

Leader: Prepare your hearts and your minds. Study to show yourselves as those worthy of God's name.

People: We will strive to be children worthy of such a great God.

19

Leader: If we would find God in our lives; if our worship is to be fulfilling; we must seek God's will for us.

People: Speak to us, Lord, as we open our ears and our hearts to your presence in our lives.

Leader: The Lord is present to those who seek him, to those who seek him in a spirit of love and humility.

People: We place our lives in your hands, O Lord. Lead us, and we will follow.

Calls to Worship

20

Leader: The Lord is near to all who call upon him in Spirit and in truth.

People: We will strive to be truth seekers, Lord, and to be attentive to your Spirit.

Leader: We are called to expand our horizons so that we understand more about God, not to create false limits so that he better fits our understanding of him.

People: We will strive to understand you better, Lord, so that we may grow in wisdom and in stature before you.

21

Leader: Seek the Lord while he may be found. Call upon him while he is near.

People: Forgive us, God, for the many times we have failed to seek you, or to seek your will for us.

Leader: Let us depart from constant busyness. Take time to listen, so that God may speak to us.

People: We are come here, Lord, in the presence of this company, to seek you. Speak to us in the silence of our hearts.

22

Leader: The Lord our God calls us to launch out into the deep waters, risking ourselves in his service.

People: Lead us, Lord. We will go wherever you send us.

Leader: We need never fear, for God will always be with us, to guide and comfort us.

People: We trust in God to bring us to a safe harbor at the end of our days. For now, we choose the open seas, willingly meeting every challenge life may bring.

23

Leader: Fear the Lord and serve him gladly.

People: How can we serve the Lord in a world gone mad?

Leader: By putting our trust in him and going forward, never looking back.

People: We will trust in him and follow him as best we can.

24

Leader: From whence comes the glory of God?

People: God is glorified when we witness to his presence by our love.

Leader: Let us, then, give ourselves in service to God so that others may see his glory.

People: With gladness of heart we serve the Lord, who has given so much to us.

25

Leader: Seek the Lord while he may be found.

People: His love empowers us to reach our full potential — as his children.

Leader: But love is not enough. God will not be found by those who will not follow him.

People: We will give the Lord first place in our lives and trust in his leading us to victory.

26

Leader: Let us return to the Lord, for with him is truth and life.

People: We gladly give ourselves to the Lord, who has given so much to us.

Leader: In his temple we find peace that the world can neither understand nor destroy.

People: In his service, we find that our lives take on new meaning and fullness.

27

Leader: Let us praise God who gives us new life.

People: We thank you, God, for taking a hand in our lives and helping us find meaning in an often meaningless world.

Leader: Let us choose God and give our lives over into his

keeping.

People: **We pledge ourselves and all that we possess to the service of your kingdom, Lord.**

28

Leader: Behold, the Lord is the light of our lives.

People: **Shine into our lives, O Lord, so that we may see the way we are to go.**

Leader: God gives light to those who desire to see, vision to those who listen when he speaks.

People: **We give ear, O Lord, to your word. Lead us where you will. We will follow.**

29

Leader: God calls us to be holy, as he is holy.

People: **We answer your call, Lord, and set our eyes upon your holiness.**

Leader: God will not leave us helpless. His Spirit will guide and uphold us, *if* we will accept his call.

People: **We accept your call, Lord, and place our lives in your hands.**

30

Leader: Seek the Lord while he may be found; call upon him while he is near.

People: **We gladly go to him when we need him.**

Leader: *Now* we need God. *Now* we must establish our relationship with him, if we hope to find him when we "need" him.

People: **Today, we will give our lives over into his keeping and seek his will for us.**

31

Leader: Wait upon the Lord, for he will surely come.

People: **When he comes, will he come in glory?**

Leader: He will surely come in glory, but only those with a heart to believe will perceive his glory.

People: Open our hearts, Lord, that we may see you with our heart's eye, and in seeing, believe.

32

Leader: Come to the Lord, whose love can cast out all our fears.

People: We trust in you, Lord, but still we approach our future with fear and trembling.

Leader: Give over your lives to the Holy Spirit. Only then will your faith be greater than your fears.

People: Enter our hearts, Lord. Make your abode with us and turn our fear into fearlessness.

33

Leader: Come, let us worship God with our whole being, holding nothing back.

People: It is difficult to go so far as to give ourselves, but we will try.

Leader: God will fill our hearts, if we will open them to his presence.

People: Here we are, Lord. Fill us with your divine love.

34

Leader: Trust in the Lord and seek his presence.

People: Our hope is in the Lord. We gladly trust in him.

Leader: Serve the Lord with gladness for, in his service, we find life.

People: Since he has given us our lives, it is only just that we should serve him.

35

Leader: It is not enough that we worship God with our hearts and lives.

People: What more do we need?

Leader: We must affirm our unity, in Christ, with all who call

God by name so that we may truly worship God in Spirit and in Truth.

People: **Help us, O Lord, to hold out our hands in fellowship to all who call on your name so that our worship will be truly acceptable to you.**

36

Leader: Behold, the King of Glory waits. Let us answer his call.

People: **Speak to us, Lord, and we will listen.**

Leader: The Lord, our Savior, has given so much to us. What shall we give in return?

People: **Take our lives, Lord, and lead us where you would have us go.**

37

Leader: Come to the Lord, who overlooks our sins.

People: **No sin is so great but that God is willing to forgive, if we are ready to repent.**

Leader: Let us serve this Lord, who has given us a great commission in his service.

People: **Service to our Lord brings joy and peace to the servant.**

38

Leader: Come — worship the Lord who gives us the victory.

People: **He lives, and because he lives, we live.**

Leader: Take up your cross and follow him who can turn that cross into a crown.

People: **We give our lives to God so that we may become new beings.**

39

Leader: Now that Easter is over, will we return to life as usual?

People: **No! Easter has made a difference in our lives, and there is no going back.**

Leader: Let us press onward then for the prize that is ours,

a life renewed in Christ.
People: **Christ has shown us the way. We will trust in him.**

40

Leader: Come, stand before the Lord who grants us victory.
People: **In his presenoe we find the strength to go on when we have thought we were finished.**
Leader: No defeat can bring us so low that his presence cannot bring us hope.
People: **We trust in him. Let the world do its worst.**

41

Leader: Let us walk in the way of the Lord.
People: **He will guide our footsteps.**
Leader: He has given us dominion over the works of his hands.
People: **Let us deal wisely and responsibly with his world.**

42

Leader: Let us praise the Lord for things, though past, that continue to fill our lives with meaning.
People: **Thank you, Lord, for showing us the way our past remains with us even now.**
Leader: God, who guided our ancestors, continues to guide us.
People: **Thank you, God, for caring enough for us to send your Son to show us the way to life.**

43

Leader: Come to the Lord, who gives wings to our words.
People: **Help us, Lord, to speak wisely to those we meet of your unchanging love.**
Leader: The Lord will empower us so that we may be witnesses to his Word.

People: **We will be a light to those who live in darkness.**

44

Leader: The Lord has spoken. How can we not obey?
People: **We hear your voice, Lord, but many other voices also clammor for our attention.**
Leader: But the Lord has spoken. How can we not obey?
People: **We hear your voice, Lord. Though it tear our hearts in two, we shall obey.**

45

Leader: Be still, so God may speak to you in the silence of your heart.
People: **We need your peace within our hearts, O Lord; there is so little within our world.**
Leader: His peace is for those who seek it, and for those who share it.
People: **We promise, Lord, to speak for peace, to spread love abroad throughout our land.**

46

Leader: Seek the Lord while he may be found; call upon him while he is near.
People: **We cast aside our self-concern, Lord, to be caught up in the joy of serving you.**
Leader: And what does the Lord require of us?
People: **To be just to all we meet; to show constant love; and to obey him.**

47

Leader: The Lord has been mindful of us; he will bless us.
People: **He will bless those who fear him, both the great and the small.**
Leader: Let us thank the Lord for his steadfast love.
People: **And for his wonderful works to those who love him.**

48

Leader: How shall we serve our blessed Lord, who has given us so much?

People: We serve him best by serving those of his children who stand in dire need.

Leader: Let us praise the Lord with our lips and our lives, walking in the way of holiness and love.

People: Thank you, God, for giving us the greatest gift, the chance to serve you and yours.

49

Leader: Why have you come?

People: We gather in the name of Jesus Christ, our Lord.

Leader: What are you doing here?

People: We gather to recall, to reaffirm, to be renewed.

Leader: Will you listen with your ears, see with your eyes, and be open in your hearts?

People: We will receive what God has for us in this hour.

50

Leader: Welcome, people of God. Are you ready to worship the Lord?

People: We are ready to worship and to praise him.

Leader: Are you willing to receive his love?

People: We open our hearts and minds to the power and influence of his love and care.

Leader: Are you humbly anticipating the freshness of his forgiveness?

People: We want to be forgiven, to know the beauty and cleanness of being restored to him.

51

Leader: God calls us to brave the darkest night.

People: When God is near we have no fear of the dark shadows that

Calls to Worship

close around us.
Leader: In his light we find sufficient illumination for our way.
People: In his love we dare to walk the stony and lonely trails of life.

52

Leader: This is the day which the Lord has made; let us rejoice and be glad in it.
People: This is not a time of sorrow but a time for joy, because our Lord is with us.
Leader: Those who worship Jahweh must worship him in spirit and in truth.
People: For he is a God of truth, and he desires us to be a spiritual people.

53

Leader: Let us worship God with songs of praise.
People: His presence fills our hearts to overflowing.
Leader: Let us worship God with our lives, serving him wherever he calls us.
People: His love is so great we have to share it. It is too good to keep for ourselves.

54

Leader: Let us rejoice that we have been found worthy of God's kingdom.
People: He has prepared a place for us, and we are his people.
Leader: In his service, every problem seems insignificant, every trouble but a fleeting instant.
People: In his service, we indeed become his people, and rise with wings of hope over the problems that surround us.

55

Leader: God is truth, and in his truth, we find light for our way.
People: As we follow him, the night becomes as day.
Leader: In his presence, we need not fear the world and its ways,

People: For God will support and sustain us in every situation.

56

Leader: Seek Jesus who is the living way.
People: The name of Jesus is precious to our lips.
Leader: Even before we seek him, God reaches out to us.
People: How can we help but respond to such love?

57

Leader: Christmas is a gift of life, a life which should be lived in gratitude.
People: We thank you, Lord, for this gift and promise to live as you would have us live.
Leader: When we truly live for God, we find joy in all our relationships, for where God is, there is peace.
People: Grant us, Lord, the courage to take up our lives, so we may know this joy and peace.

58

Leader: Let us praise God for the change Christmas has made in our lives.
People: Thank you, Lord, for Christ, and for the love he showers on our lives.
Leader: But let us thank God with our lives, and not just our lips.
People: We promise to reach for the joy of Christmas, and to share the joy with everyone we meet.

59

Leader: Behold, we are a convenant people!
People: God's chosen, children of the most high God.
Leader: We are his people,
People: If we abide in our covenant as true children of righteousness.

Calls to Worship

60

Leader: Come and let us learn of God!
People: We seek his guidance for our lives this day and for the days to come.
Leader: In him we live and move and have our being.
People: In him, our lives take on meaning, and our joy is full.

61

Leader: Sing praise to God who reigns above.
People: His love is a shelter in the storm and a light in the darkness.
Leader: His presence directs our lives, if we will listen to him.
People: We will indeed listen to him, and we will go where he leads us.

62

Leader: Come, all who seek strength to face the coming days; in return to and rest in the Lord you will find strength.
People: Bless us with your presence, Lord, that we may continue in the way that has been set before us.
Leader: Give thanks to God who knows our needs before we even speak.
People: Thank you, God, for being you, for being near to see us through.

63

Leader: If you desire to be a people of vision, come to the Lord, who gives freely to those who earnestly seek.
People: We come to you, O Lord. Open our eyes and our hearts so that we may indeed be a people of vision.
Leader: Seek also wisdom, for without wisdom all visions are empty and useless.
People: Open our eyes and our minds, O Lord, so that we may understand what we see.

64

Leader: Let us praise God who sought us out while we were yet sinners.

People: His love has enabled us to take hold of life.

Leader: Let us praise God by being instruments of his will.

People: By reaching out in love to those the world is unable to love.

65

Leader: God is here! Let us celebrate his presence.

People: With God's help we will make our whole life a celebration.

Leader: God is here! Let us pledge our love to him.

People: In love, we give our lives to him, to do with as he pleases.

66

Leader: *Now* is the day of salvation! *Now* we are called to serve God!

People: We will answer when he calls. We will go where he sends us.

Leader: Good News is meant to be shared.

People: We will seek to know his will so that we can share him with everyone.

67

Leader: Surely, God is worthy of praise.

People: Shout hosannas and proclaim his glory to the ends of the earth.

Leader: Come before him and bring gifts worthy of his great glory.

People: With what shall we come to the Lord of Hosts, the great God of the universe?

Leader: With justice, mercy, and acts of love, even towards those who least deserve them.

People: So be it.

Calls to Worship

68

Leader: Sing praises to God who reigns above and within the hearts of those who follow him.

People: He is ever present to comfort and to guide us.

Leader: We can safely trust in God to sustain us and to make our lives worth living.

People: His peace keeps our hearts and minds joyful, because we are in tune with his universe.

69

Leader: Let us rejoice in the blessings God has given us.

People: He has given us many gifts in order that we might live abundantly.

Leader: Let us cherish these gifts and use them wisely.

People: Amen. With patience and true godliness, we must pursue those policies which will insure that our gifts will not be squandered.

70

Leader: Come to the Christ, all who labor and are heavy laden, and he will give you rest.

People: We praise God for those who share our burdens with us.

Leader: Take his yoke upon you, for it is not a yoke of shame but of forgiving love.

People: Gladly do we share in his ministry to this dark and lonely world.

Part 2

Prayers of Confession

Prayers of Confession

1

Eternal God, your grace is sufficient for all our needs. When we are open to your Holy Spirit, we are sustained in our attempt to live as followers of Christ. The problem is that, once we get started on the road to salvation, we are often tempted to give ourselves more credit than we deserve. The farther along we go the more puffed up we become. We even think we deserve your favor because of all that we have done for you and for your kingdom. Forgive our foolish pride, Lord, and teach us not to count on our great deeds but to depend on your grace, in our struggle to be the people you created us to be. Amen

2

We hear your Word, O Lord, but we are slow to obey. So many other voices call out to us. We hear the siren call of the world, and we waver in our intentions. And even if we do not waver, we behold how poorly others respond to our ministry, and we get discouraged. Forgive us, Lord, for our wavering. Sustain us when we waver or are discouraged. Do not take away your presence, but stir our hearts so that we may take courage and take up the tasks to which you call us. May we never disgrace your Holy Spirit. Amen

3

O Lord, you promise us salvation. To all who leave behind their old lives you promise new. We are joyful to receive new lives for old, but we are not willing to pay the price. We can always find a church which will promise us the new life at a cheap price. But there is no "cheap grace." There is always a cross awaiting those who choose the new life you offer. Give us the courage to put Christ first and to invest our lives in the task of preparing the way for your kingdom. May we never be content with a status quo based on injustice and

Prayers of Confession

falsehood. May our hearts and lives be filled with your Holy Spirit, so we may have your peace within our lives. Amen

4

O God, sometimes we act as if we had never heard of Jesus, except as a peg on which to hang our own twisted thoughts. Rather than listening to him we follow the dictates of our own hearts, all the while *claiming* to do what we do in his name. Nowhere is this more evident than in our refusal to seek out the sinner or to seek to heal the wounds which are so evident in our world. Our ways are so tame in comparison to his. No one would think of crucifying us because we take the "safe" road of personal religion and allow the world to enslave the hearts and minds of people. No radical religion for us, that requires speaking out against injustice. Why do we fail to follow you, God? Have mercy on us and turn us from our foolish ways. Amen

5

We read in the Bible, Lord, of the many times you came to the aid of your chosen people, but the past seems so far away and the present is so filled with problems. We know in our head that we can trust your promise to come to us in our hour of need, but deep inside, where our feelings are, we feel so alone that our heart won't listen to our head. Help us, Lord, to trust in our reasons for trusting you, so that slowly we may come to an awareness of your holy presence within us, offering us the guidance we need in these dark days. Grant us, also, the courage to continue our quest for your kingdom and a sense of humor so that we may keep things in proper perspective. Amen

6

God, we know that our lives often do not measure up to the possibilities we have in Christ. We are prone to admire violent and arrogant men (although only so long as they cater to our perverse desires). We make commitments, but, like Peter, we back out when the going gets hard. Forgive us, Lord. Enable us, like Peter, at last to conquer our fear and carry the challenge of your kingdom into the very heart of the pagan capitals of the world (including our own). Amen

7

We confess, Dear Lord, that we have played the Pharisee, refusing to believe in love designed to set your people free. The Bible speaks eloquently of your love for the poor and the outcast, but still we live within our narrow way, with awe for the rich and contempt for the poor, and you will seldom find us "wasting" time with those who stand outside our faith, with those who will not obey the rules that we have set down. Forgive us, Lord, and teach us to respond with love to everyone we meet, refusing to accept the barriers our ancestors placed between people, or even those our society insists on erecting from time to time. May we instead build bridges of love. Amen

8

We gladly follow you, Lord, for in your service we find life. Many voices speak to us, saying, "Follow," but they lead to blind alleys. Only in your service are our eyes and hearts opened. The only problem is that we are sometimes tempted to pretend to more knowledge of you and your will then we really have. Worse, when we do this, we seem to do it for the purpose of limiting you to *our* concerns. We see Jesus as Messiah, but as *our* Messiah, and expect him to place us in positions of power. Forgive us for our narrow vision and our sometimes limited love. Help us to expand our vision and our love until we are worthy children of such a great God. Amen

Prayers of Confession

9

O God, you have given us many gifts. Our very lives are lived in the shadow of your love. Nothing that befalls us is able to separate us from that love, for your love is stronger than all the forces of evil. Forgive us when we doubt the power of your love and trust, instead, in weapons of oppression and war. Help us to dare to live victorious lives in the midst of defeat, joyful lives in the midst of sorrow. In all things may our lives bear witness to the power and the presence of your love. Amen

10

O God, you have called us to forgive everyone in the same way that you forgave us, and yet we find it so difficult to forgive others, especially when it seems to us that they are breaking important laws that you have commanded. In our zeal for your kingdom, we forget that it can only be entered by those who have a loving and forgiving heart. Help us, Lord, to remember that love is more important than zeal, and that no doctrine is so important that we are right in blindly enforcing it without attempting to understand and love the person we are concerned about. Help us to realize that people are always more important than doctrines, and that, if we have not love, we "are nothing." Amen

11

Eternal God, our loving Lord, we who know of your power and glory ought to tell others of your way that leads to abundant life and peace. You have given us, as Christ's disciples, the task of turning people away from the idols that blind them to the waywardness of their lives, and to the hope for renewal that you hold out to them. We know that we have not always taken up our responsibility. We profess a policy of live and let live that would let our brothers and sisters continue on their way to damnation. Encourage us, Lord, as we try to proclaim your living way to a people who are sometimes so lost that they don't even know they are lost, and help us to always do this with a loving and patient heart. In Jesus' name we pray. Amen

12

O God, Christmas proclaims to us your presence, and promises us that we are never far from you, and that you offer us peace. But we have preferred platitudes to your peace, and in place of the good will you ask us to show one another, we have practiced deceit and contempt. Forgive us, Lord. Teach us to live in such a way that Christmas will be a part of our lives every day of the year. Amen

13

We are like the second son, O Lord, the one who talked a good fight but who wasn't there when it counted. We make great promises to you, and we mean them, but something always seems to get in the way — friends from out of town we have to entertain; a field that needs plowing or harvesting; that good time we have been promising ourselves. Forgive us, Lord. Send some shock waves through the quietude of our piety so that we may see ourselves as we truly are: children who have been straying from the path of righteousness. Amen

14

O God, our loving Lord, you give freely to all who turn to you. Too often, we try to add conditions to your grace. Refusing to accept people with the unconditional love that is your hallmark, we place burdens on them that are too heavy to bear. We have also developed a hierarchy of values for judging people. We value those who have a long history of serving you, but only tolerate (and sometimes not even that) those people who come to us with a sordid past. We do not see clearly because we do not see with the eyes of love. Cleanse our hearts, Lord, so that we may begin to love with the same

Prayers of Confession

love that you have shown us, a love that meets people at their point of need, without raising up unnecessary barriers. Amen

15

O Lord, you have called us to be a living sacrifice, dedicated to your service, conforming ourselves not to this world, but allowing ourselves to be transformed by the renewal of our minds. We have resisted such a radical demand on our lives, giving countless excuses for our unwillingness to change. Forgive us, God. Enable us, by your gracious presence, to perceive the possibilities for life around us, so that we may choose life rather than death. In Jesus' name we pray. Amen

16

You planted us so joyfully, O Lord, and cared so tenderly for our needs, and we have returned your grace by forming closed communities, setting your teeth on edge. With loving care you formed us. You appointed prophets and priests to teach us your will and your way, but we, like sheep, have gone astray. We ignore fundamental instructions that Jesus and Paul gave us, while fastening on matters of trivia and creating iron-clad rules from them that make religion a burden rather than a joy. Forgive us our foolishness, Lord. Teach us to hang loose and follow Christ of Galilee rather than the Pharisees of Jerusalem. Amen

17

You have given us new life, O Lord. For such a great gift, we should be ever thankful, yet we quickly take it for granted. We see our lives in terms of special privileges, and forget our responsibilities. We assume that judgment is for other people, not us, and so we look forward to the day we stand before you. We assume that it will be an easy time, but Jesus and the prophets warn us that it will be a time of trial for those who will not risk themselves in God's service. Forgive us, Lord, for neglecting to use our gifts for your glory, for thinking only of ourselves. Help us to be like those who turned privilege into action, thinking not about the risks they were taking, but only desiring to benefit their Lord. May we, too, work for your glory. Amen

18

O God, you come to us while we are seeking other gods, and you call us to return to you. You are always ready to deliver us from the pit of despair or the tentacles of pride. Forgive us when we seek release through drugs or through following other gods, gods of iron and stone, which have no power to deliver us. Create us anew in your image so that we might become a whole and holy community once more. Amen

19

O Lord, why do we never learn? Before Christ came, religion was more of a burden than a blessing. The Pharisees took more pride in their rules and their appearances as "pious people" than in being a "light to the Gentiles," so that they too might know of your power and your love. Christ proclaimed a way of loving service to everyone, a way of forgetting ourselves in our service to those who presently stand outside your love. Can we honestly say that we follow Christ's command to love others as we love ourselves, that we gladly choose service over show? Like the Pharisees, we love our rules and our privileges. Like them, we like to make it clear who are the good guys and who are the bad guys. The appearance of piety is more important than the reality. Forgive us, Lord. Help us as we seek to be the people Christ freed us to be, a people for whom forgiveness is more important than favors, serving than being served, loving than being loved. In the name of him who gave his life for many. Amen

20

O Gracious God, we have no hope apart from you, for in you we find life. You desire that all your children live abundant lives. We are grateful for the concern that you show for us,

Prayers of Confession

and for the joyful life that is ours when we live as your children. Our problem is that we often have a limited view of what it means to be your children. We see our privileges clearly, but our responsibilities only dimly. It is not that we actively pursue evil where your other children are concerned. Rather, we do nothing. At times, we even go to great effort to keep ourselves ignorant of the many needs of people around us. Forgive us, Lord. Teach us not to trust in our static righteousness but to seek to live quiet lives of love. May we find no service to you or your children beneath our dignity. Amen

21

Lord, God of the universe, yours is the power from everlasting to everlasting. You strengthen us when we are weak and comfort us when we are sorrowing. Turn to us now in our distress. We do not know where our world is going, and we are afraid to find out, so we go through life with blinders on, afraid of what we might see. We talk much about religion, but when it comes to doing something about it, we find plenty of excuses for doing nothing. Some people give up in despair; others find solace in an escapist religion, waiting for you to come and personally straighten things out. Forgive us, Lord, and teach us that patience which enables us to creatively "wait on the Lord," waiting not with quiet hands but with hands ready to serve you now. Amen

22

O Lord, we know that you have called us to be your chosen people. We realize that it is a great honor, and we cherish our relationship with you. However, we are tempted by people who have a certain charisma to give our first loyalty to them, at least in everything that counts. We may give lip service to your rule in our lives, but we only listen to you through them. Forgive us, Lord. Open our hearts and our ears so that we may hear you and abide in your love. Teach us to treasure you above all earthly leaders and to follow you wherever you call us to go. Amen

23

We know, O Lord, that you have accepted us, even though we often do things which try your patience. We also know that we are quicker to follow the world's way of accepting people only "on approval" than we are to follow your way of unconditional acceptance. Forgive us, Lord, for being closed and judgmental when we should be open and accepting. Help us so that we may learn to value your wisdom over the wisdom of the world. Amen

24

You promise us new life, Lord, but we take too much for granted and become lazy, and even arrogant. We take pride in gifts we have received from you as if we had achieved them through great effort on our part. We see no necessity for disciplined study to prepare us for whatever the future may bring, and thus we often find ourselves unprepared to deal with unpleasant situations. Instead of facing up to the responsibility to live our faith, we rationalize our failures. Forgive us, Lord. Touch us with your healing grace and teach us the wisdom of always being prepared, of using periods of peace to prepare ourselves for those times we may be called on to perform unfamiliar or unpleasant tasks. May we never give you cause to be ashamed of us. Amen.

25

O God, you have called us to be part of a great people, a holy priesthood consecrated to the service of your kingdom. You have given us many gifts, whereby we are able to create a place where you are worshipped and where people live together in harmony and prosperity. We confess that we have not done our part in making your dream for the world a reality. Forgive those fears and jealousies which cause us to

Prayers of Confession

"look out for number one." Give us the wisdom and courage to join with your children everywhere in one great effort to tell people of your unchangeable love. Amen

26

O Lord, our gracious God, you have given us life. You have chosen to bless us with many gifts, gifts that enable us to serve you and to make this world a fit place for our children and our grandchildren. Help us, Lord, as we seek to use these gifts wisely. Temptations to use these gifts for our own benefit, and not yours, often lead us astray. Spread your love abroad in our hearts and our land, and guide us as we seek to be a people with a divine purpose: the sharing of your Gospel and your Law. Amen

27

O Lord, you have given us great gifts, and you have commissioned us to use these gifts for the advancement of your kingdom. Many, like Cyrus, use your gifts for the work of the kingdom but never know of your glory or give you the credit you deserve. They march victorious to the grave, but ever ignorant of the greatness of their calling. Others know themselves as your children, and do not waste their lives in "riotous living," but they *do* waste their lives in "religious living," a living that knows many of the right words but produces nothing of any practical value for your kingdom. Help us to be like the people of Thessalonica, whose faith in the Good News of Christ's love led them to practical activities, whose love led them to undertake joyfully even the most menial and toilsome labors, and whose hope helped them stand firm in the face of their trials. Amen

28

Eternal God, our gracious Lord, we gladly accept the gift of new life you hold out to us, and we are proud to be a part

Prayers of Confession

of the new community you have created in Christ. However, we are much slower to accept the tasks that go with the new life. You have created us anew and given us your Holy Spirit, so that we may be fathers and mothers in Christ to those who still dwell in darkness, so that they may come to the light which is Christ. Forgive us, Lord, when our thoughts are too often about ourselves, and what we may obtain, and too seldom about those who are lost in loneliness and despair, and what we may do to bring the light of Christ into their joyless lives. Guide us by your love as we try to live up to the great potential that is ours as your childran, of being light for the blind and joy for those locked in sorrow. Amen

29

Our gracious God, you created us for fellowship with you and so that we might serve you by making rough places plain, making this a better world for your children. We have often failed in this task, even after you sent Christ to free us from the sins which bound us fast. He freed us, but we still prefer the snug harbor of our sins to the open seas of life where problems often seem overwhelming. Forgive us our fears, Lord, and grant us the courage that cares enough to give of our very best in service to you and to our world. May we find our peace in the wholeness of lives spent in your service, rather than in the quietude of empty lives. Amen

30

Eternal God, creator and preserver of the universe, you have chosen us to be your agents in the creation of your kingdom, soldiers in your army of love, priests to heal the wounds of your children, and prophets to offer the guidance of your wisdom to those lost in despair. We have repaid such love by building walls between us and those we were called to save. We rest content with empty worship that caters to our prejudices without challenging us to enlarge our world. We see you as the preserver of *our* values, the defender of *our*

Prayers of Confession

faith. We have sought to capture you in brick and mortar, limiting you to *our* church. We are more concerned with the purity of our beliefs and the upkeep of our buildings than with the performance of our duty of love. Forgive us, Lord, for hoarding your gifts for our own benefit. Help us to realize that it is in giving of ourselves that we receive. Teach us to build bridges of love rather than walls and to take the risk of caring for others. Amen

31

Our Lord, our God, we have not lived up to the glorious heritage which is ours. When we have looked to the past, it was often with the purpose of deifying it in order that we might avoid the challenges of the present. We have not seen our heritage as a springboard to better service to you and to one another, but as an albatross about our neck to remind us of past errors, or as something to which we owed blind allegiance. Help us, O Lord, to follow the example of Paul by forgetting that which is past and pressing on to the goal of the prize which is God's call through Jesus Christ to life. Amen

32

It is me, O Lord, who is in need of prayer and the confidence that you know and hear my prayer. So I turn to you now with my troubles and all of the ups and downs of my life. You know me on the inside. You know *all* my feelings, and I dare to hope that you understand them all and accept me as I now am. I confess that sometimes my life is rich with meaning and confidence in you, but at other times I falter and stumble and find myself a contributor to the cruelties and prejudices which break down and destroy relationships. Lord, make me an instrument of your peace; where there is hatred, let me sow love; where there is injury, pardon; where there is sadness, joy. Amen

Prayers of Confession

33

God, we hear of people and their needs, and yet we are not moved to pity. We accuse them of being lazy, or we assert that they do not deserve our help. And yet, Lord, you have helped us, and we did not deserve your help. You have loved us, even when we didn't deserve your love, because you are a loving God. Open our eyes, so that we may see that everyone we meet is our brother or sister, because they have been created by you. Help us to become a loving people so that we may truly participate in your divine nature and share in your eternal kingdom. Amen

34

Leader: O God, you have given us the highest position in your chain of life, with great intellect and power over all other forms of life,

People: But we have misused our minds and have used our intellect to devise weapons to destroy life rather than to upbuild it.

Leader: O God, you have given us eyes to see the beauty of the world around us,

People: But we see only the mess that we have made of our world as we have misused it.

Leader: O God, you have given us ears so that we might hear the melody of voices and the sounds of nature,

People: But we hear only the noise of the clamoring crowd or the discords of the machines of our industrial world.

Leader: O God, you have given us hands so that we might be able to touch and feel the marvelous things around us,

People: But, as we touch these things, we realize the instability of our society and the shoddiness of much that we have made.

Leader: O God, you have given us lips to speak your praises and to offer words of love and encouragement to others,

People: But we use your name only in curses, and we speak words of bitterness and hatred to others.

Leader: O God, you have created us with the ability to smell

Prayers of Confession

the fragrance of the flowers and plants of beauty.

People: **But we smell only the foul odors of the air that we have polluted, in our haste to produce and become rich through the manufacture of things.**

Leader: O God, you have created us to enjoy freedom, with the ability to choose as we desire,

People: **But we lack a true sense of freedom, for we are bound by our sins and our complexes.**

Leader: O God, you have sent Christ to offer his life for our sins, to redeem us from the bondage of life.

People: **Make us new creatures in Christ, O Father, and guide us so that we might find peace and joy as we use our abilities as you have intended us to do. Amen**

35

O God, we are aware of your wisdom, majesty and power, and we recognize you as the creator of the universe. Still, when our problems press in upon us, we are tempted to trust in the power of our own arm or in the might of our country, rather than in you. We understand little, and desire less, the power of self-sacrifice which you offer us. We believe it pays to be nice, until we want to be first in something, and then we act as if we believe that "nice guys finish last." Success, and not the cross, leads us on. We find sacrifice difficult, because we have not been taught to love "everyone." We may "tolerate" those who do not love us, but love is hard. Forgive us, God. Give us the courage to trust in you and in your power, and the way of the cross. Free us from our fears by the power of your love. Amen

36

O Lord, we hear Christ, but only dimly, and nowhere as dimly as when he calls us to love our enemies. We rationalize his words and live by the law of tooth and claw. We seldom surprise those who injure us with the reponse of love, as Christ said we must do. Our responses are all too typical of "normal" human responses: we react with hate and vengeance, never even thinking of turning the other cheek. Forgive us, Lord; we are but children and do not know what we are doing. Help us to conquer our hate. Enable us to become loving persons, as Christ was and as he called us to be. Amen

37

Leader: When all seems lost, Lord, and we are afraid to begin again,

People: Forgive us, and inspire our hearts with hope.

Leader: When all our problems seem insurmountable,

People: Give us the courage to carry on with our daily living.

Leader: When we think only of self and seek only our own good, refusing to work with, or have concern for, others,

People: Help us to see that our strength is in our union, and that only as we work together in your name can we hope to solve our problems.

Leader: When we are tempted to put immediate gain ahead of the wise use of the rich resources you have given us,

People: Grant us the wisdom to see the error of our ways and the courage to repent.

Leader: When we are in danger of losing faith in our country or of making our country an idol that we worship,

People: Help us to see that "our help comes from the Lord," and that our nation can rise to greater glory only as we trust in you and commit ourselves to actions we truthfully believe to be worthy.

38

O God, we hear your call to us. We know that you love us. However, we are too easily satisfied with merely knowing that you love us and that we are your children. We fail to search out the full meaning of this wonderful news for our everyday lives. Thus we endanger our souls — by neglecting to be the kind of people you insist on your children being. Forgive us, Lord. Break down the walls of our satisfaction with less than our best. Inspire us to give our all in service to you and to

Prayers of Confession

those who need us, so that we may find that abundant life reserved for those who know how to be your children fully and completely. Amen

39

O God, our gracious Lord, we pray your forgiveness for our blind and selfish ways. We close our eyes to our friends' lies and distortions of the truth, because we do not want to make the sacrifice of living as you would have us live. We wink at faults we ought to condemn, and excuse those acts even more the more people we find doing them. We fail to perceive the connection between our actions, or failures to act, and gross injustices perpetuated by our society, because we do not want to acknowledge our guilt. Help us, God. Open our eyes that we may see, our hearts that we may love, and our minds that we may have the wisdom to live. In Jesus' name we pray. Amen

40

God, we desire life, but often we settle for a slow death instead, because we fear the unknown more than we desire life. To live is such a risky business because it invites us to leap before we know where we are going — and we have always been taught to "look before we leap," to play it safe. Our eyes are too dim and our wits too dull to see the glory of the life you offer, and we don't have the courage to leave behind our certainties. Forgive us, Lord. Help us to see with the eyes of faith, to dare hope when all seems hopeless or when we are only dimly aware of the future, and to dare to love before we are loved, so that we might enter your kingdom now, in the land of the living. Amen

41

God, you speak to us in many ways, but we are prone to listen only to the voices we understand, and our choice is often poor. Words that could save us are not heard because we scorn their lowly orign. People remain our enemies because we turn aside from countless opportunities to reach out to them in love. Cure us of our blindness, Lord, and lead us along your path of love to fullness of life. Amen

42

O God, you hold out to us the possibility of wholeness, the possibility of people learning to live in peace — if only we would lay aside our pride and prejudice. But we so quickly become wrapped up in the dead letter of human laws and doctrines, protecting our past rather than living in the present. We ignore blatant evils that cry out to us for redress. We turn people away from our churches and our homes, because they are not the right race, color, or creed. Forgive us, Lord. Fill us with your love so that we are only able to see Christ in those whom we meet, not their differences from us. May we become a community in the fullest sense of the word, so that by our love for one another we may draw others to you. Amen

43

Gracious Lord, out of your love for us, you have given us freely of yourself, holding nothing back, hoping thereby to teach us to live openly with one another, sharing our joys and our sorrows. And yet, so often, Lord, we fail to live up to the great promise that is ours. Not only do we fail to love our enemies; we also fail to love our friends. We use the freedom you have given us to avoid our responsibilities and to advance our own selfish causes. Forgive us, Lord, and lead us by your great love into paths of righteousness and responsibility. Amen

44

We hear your call, Lord, but, like Elijah, we are fearful of the Jezebels who wield power in our land. In fear, we run and hide. In piety, we call for you to come and set things right. It would be a good time for you to come, Lord. We often feel over-

Prayers of Confession

whelmed by the problems facing us. Grant us courage, Lord, so that we may live out our faith, leaving our caves for hiding to those who do not know our Lord, Jesus, your Son, who set for us the example of a life obedient unto death. Amen

45

O God, we feel your presence close to us, and we are moved to witness to the meaning of your presence for our lives. So often, though, we are either too timid or too arrogant. In some situations we are so fearful we say nothing. At other times, we control people in a way no one has a right to control another person. We tend to dictate to people how they may experience you and how they may serve you. If people are in need of help, we offer help, but often we put strings on our help, strings which any self-respecting persons would refuse. Lord, forgive us our blindness to the uniqueness of people. Help us to accept their ways of differing from us and to witness to your love in a dynamic way whereby we are neither derelict in our duty nor manipulative with our love. Amen.

46

Eternal God, we who have hesitated before life's uncertainties pray that you will forgive us our cowardice and wash away our fears. Your promise of abundant life is limited only because we, your children, have often taken the easy road of non-involvement, rather than the sometimes stormy road of concern for the problems of your people. Create in us a desire for the abundant life you promised, so that together we can make this world livable for us and and for all your children. Amen.

47

O God, in your unsearchable wisdom, you chose to make us co-creators with you, yet we have met this great challenge with a pious refusal to aspire to roles we consider "too great" for us, or with an arrogant using of our creativity and freedom to enslave others for our benefit. Forgive us, God, and help us to meet the challenge to live creatively as followers of Christ, being neither timid nor arrogant but living up to the best that is in us, counting neither the cost nor the gain but simply glorying in your name. Amen

11/26/89

48

Merciful Father, you never come to us without mystery, and you never leave us without hope. Forgive us when our actions show how little we trust you. Forgive our impatience when good is slow to conquer evil; forgive our closemindedness when we think we know all about your love; forgive our bitterness when we don't get all the love we feel we need. When we grow too attached to familiar things, put us on a new road, a road of challenging service to you; when pride takes the place of gratitude, show us your unexpected blessing. Have mercy on us, Lord Jesus, when you leave us behind to serve you but we forget why we are called your people. Amen

49

O God, you sent Jesus to call us to unburden ourselves of the chains that bind us to outmoded and harmful ways of interacting; but in our foolishness we often cling to the very modes of actions which prevent us from being free. We choose enslavement to the past rather than openness to the future; darkness rather than light; ignorance rather than knowledge; and isolation rather than community with Christ and others, which has the power to bring us abundant life. Forgive us, God, and enable us to affirm the life which you have given us. Amen

50

O Lord, forgive us when we go astray and refuse to hear your Word to us. Our desires tempt us sorely when we see others

Prayers of Confession

enjoying things we wish we had, or doing things we wish we had time to do, and we are often tempted to try to "keep up with the Joneses." The call to duty falls but dimly on our ears at such times, and we are inclined to sulk at your continual and urgent call to our consciences to be about your business. Enable us to follow your will for us joyfully, so that our lives may be full and abundant. In Jesus' name we pray. Amen

51

You have created us, Lord, and you have called us your children in a special way that we have a hard time understanding. Help us to make sense of our calling. You have given us a ministry to perform in your name, and you have given us Christ, as an example of how we should be, and to help us become what we are capable of becoming. But there are many other voices that we listen to, voices that are very tempting because they urge us to take the easy way and to shun the cross, which always sheds its shadow over our pathway. Help us, Lord, to follow in Christ's steps, so that we may know the joy that only comes from serving you. Amen

52

O God, you have loved us with a great love. Though we deserved condemnation, you gave us forgiving love. Yet, we have repaid your great love by sitting in judgment over your children when they desperately needed our forgiving love. We have resorted to the lash of the whip or the lash of our tongue in order to "bring people into line." How you must sorrow over us, Lord, to see how we have forgotten how Christ reached out to us in love, not condemnation. Cleanse our hearts so that we may hear your call to follow *your* way of love rather than *our* way of force, so that peace and love may reign between your children. Amen

58

We know, O Lord, that you have called us to be holy, but the world presses in on us, making demands that seem impossible, if we are to remain true to you. We are also crushed, Lord, by a sense of impending doom. Our world seems intent on destroying itself. We are threatened on all sides by forces over which we seem to have no control, and we are tempted to give in to despair and join forces with the world in looking out only for ourselves. Forgive us, Lord. Inspire us by your Holy Word to place our lives in your hands so that we might indeed stay young and strong like an eagle, and might thereby be a positive force in making this a better world. Amen

59

O Lord, you light up our lives and make plain the path before us, if we have the faith to look and the eyes to see. However, our eyes are often dazzled by the sights of this world, and we are tempted to follow paths of our own creation, paths of arrogance and ignorance. Forgive us our foolishness, Lord. Open our eyes so that we may see the error of our willful ways, give us the courage to admit it when we are going the wrong way, and give us the wisdom to seek your way, so that our faith may once again be strengthened by your guidance in our lives. Amen

60

We give ourselves, O Lord, into your keeping. We intend to hold back nothing, but we know there will be times when we will not serve you as we should, and that there will be times when we think we are serving you but are serving Satan instead. We find it tempting to use Satan's methods to achieve your will, for in this world, Satan's methods often seem more effective. Forgive us, Lord. Help us realize we cannot achieve your will by using Satan's methods. Give us the strength of character which will enable us to serve you in the way you expect to be served. Amen

Prayers of Confession

61

O Lord, you have created us and endowed us with great possibilities. You have set us over your creation and trusted us to do what was best for the world, for ourselves, and for those who come after us. Like so many of our ancestors, we have often failed to do what we ought to have done, or have done things we knew would harm the world and deprive those who come after us of their rightful inheritance. Forgive us, Lord. Cleanse our hearts with your healing presence so that we may see clearly the choices that lie before us, and encourage us by your loving presence to give of our best in the effort to make the world more livable, to insure sufficient goods for all your children, and to give a good account of our stewardship in your name. Amen

62

We read, O Lord, where Jesus reached out to the Samaritan woman, but we don't realize how radical was the nature of that little act. We do not realize that the gulf between a Jew (especially a Rabbi) and a Samaritan (especially a woman of low repute) is like the gulf between us and our worst enemy. We continue, as did the Israelites of old, to label "our" enemies "your" enemies, so that we can continue to mistreat them without feeling guilty. Forgive us, Lord. Teach us to treasure everyone we meet as part of your creation, and therefore worthy of our love and fellowship. Amen

63

O Lord, you have created us to be your children in a world that needs our witness to your love. Instead, when people look at us, they often see arrogance, which masquerades as piety and places burdens too heavy to bear. Forgive us, Lord, when we allow our pride at being your "chosen ones" to blind us to the fact that we are still ordinary people, with quite ordinary sins and weaknesses. Help us to humbly serve your

kingdom as forgiven sinners who hold out to other sinners the promise of your forgiving love. Amen

64

O Lord of our heart, our lips confess our need for your saving grace. Protect us from that pride which would lead us to pretend that we have no need of you, that we have no need of one another. The world tries to convince us that only when we win can we know that you are near to us and care for us, and we are tempted to believe. Even people of piety would convince us, if they could, that nothing but victory comes to those who follow you. But we have tasted defeat, Lord. We know what it is to lose. Help us to seek your presence in our losses, so that even in defeat we may bless your holy name, so that even in defeat we may find a blessing. Amen

65

We hear, O Lord, Christ's call to obedience to your name, but such obedience often leads to suffering in this world. Despite the brave front we put up, fear is still able to lead us astray. We need your presence, Lord, to still our fears and to lead us back from the abyss of indifference and the chaos called pride. Only when we deliver our lives over to you are we able to face our foes with stout hearts and steadfast determination. Depart not from us, Lord, but lead us through the valley of temptation so that we may emerge on the other side victorious children of the Most High God. Amen

66

O Lord, you gave us the gift of your Holy Spirit. Forgive us if we have neglected your gift and gone our own way, depending on ourselves, or on others equally blind. Too often we are only blind guides, leading others as blind as ourselves. Such is the price we pay when we neglect your gifts, especially the gift of the Holy Spirit. Forgive us, Lord. Speak to our hearts,

Prayers of Confession

so that we may become a prepared people, able to see visions and ready to proclaim your living presence to this world of ours, which is so in need of a word of hope. Amen

67

We thank you, Lord, for the gift of faith, for the power of the Holy Spirit to cast out those fears which twist our lives into knots. And yet we still let fear of our enemies, and even our friends, too often prevent us from taking actions we believe the Holy Spirit is calling us to take. It is hard to stand against those we fear, and even harder to stand against those we admire, especially when our stand may cause us to lose their friendship. Still, we feel a compulsion within our hearts to proclaim your message, no matter how bitter it may seem to those who hear it. Sustain us by your Holy Spirit within us, Lord, or we will never have the courage to complete the course that you have set before us. Amen

68

You are a God of love, Lord, and we are your children. You are the center of our lives, and we desire to be worthy of your love. Sometimes, in our zeal for you, we forget that you *are* a God of love, and we think to use our anger in your service. Or, when others act out their anger in your name, we admire their "sincerity," and overlook the fact that anger does not work righteousness, that what we cannot win in love, we cannot win. Help us, Lord, to learn the lesson that Christ tried to teach his disciples, that only those who live lives of love are winners, that people who love always win, even when they lose, for those who love participate in your divinity. Amen

69

Leader 1: Christmas is not just a baby in a manger.
Leader 2: It is Golgotha.
People: Yet we have made Christmas a time of sentimental

nostalgia.

Leader 1: Beneath the tinsel and the bright lights stands a cross.

Leader 2: Only in that cross is suffering transformed into joy.

People: **But we seek joy in a flight from the cross and the suffering it calls us to bear.**

Leader 1: The cross calls us to live in the world as children of God,

Leader 2: To give it the best that we have, indeed to transform the world and ourselves into Christ's image.

People: **But we seek to live in two worlds, giving our allegiance to two masters, letting neither world interfere with the other.**

Leader 1: God comes to us as a God of surprises.

Leader 2: Even when we are prepared for him, we may not recognize him.

People: **But we like the ways we are accustomed to and demand of God that he conform to our expectations.**

Leader 1: Christ is our judge, as well as our Savior, and he will test us when he comes.

Leader 2: But it is Christ who is our judge, and he does not willingly afflict or condemn us.

People: **Forgive us, Lord. Fill our lives with your presence so that we may live on the growing edge of life and not in narrow life-denying ruts.**

Leader 1: It is God who calls us, and his name is "Love." He will not easily abandon us to our self-destroying ways.

70

O Lord, as Christmas approaches, we should be joyful, for Christmas proclaims the promise of hope where we now are hopeless, joy where we now have sorrow, love where we now know only hate. Yet it is hard for this promise to stir our hearts. We are too fond of hating our enemies to want to start loving them. Even our sorrow and our hopelessness give us a strange sort of satisfaction. Forgive us, Lord. Set our hearts free by your great love, so that we may not only experience the joy of Christmas in our lives, but may help others discover that joy. Amen

Prayers of Confession

71

Why is it, Lord, that Christmas can be so quickly forgotten? Is it because the presents we share are not given from the heart? Is it because we use fancy words that sound impressive but don't really touch us where we live? Indeed, we do seem to like fancy things so much that we pay a lot of attention to our places of worship, creating grand buildings that are admired by many people. We also develop worship services that would impress an emperor. But would they impress Christ? Would he commend us for our magnificent buildings or our impressive services? Or would he ask us, "Have you served your neighbor in his need?" Are our fancy frills a disguise to hide from others, and ourselves, a great lack of love within? Forgive us, Lord, for being so concerned with outward show that we don't have, or take, the time to check our spiritual pulse, or to nourish our soul. Teach us rather to cherish that simple love that looks upon the heart and not outward appearances. Amen

72

O Lord, Christmas holds a special spot within our lives. We worship with our families and find tranquility within our hearts. Why can't that feeling last, Lord? It only stays awhile and disappears, and we become as we were before the holiday: a people filled with fear and anxiety, troubled over many things. Perhaps we lack the discipline that marked the lives of Christ and Paul. We want the gifts of Christmas, but without the cross that Christ promised to those who follow him. Help us, Lord, to seek within the pages of our sacred book for words that have the power to touch our souls and to set them on fire with that divine love which can console our hearts and set us free for life and love. Amen

73

We love the Christmas story, Lord. Our hearts respond with

Prayers of Confession

joy as we sing of how the Christ child was born in Bethlehem, and how that great event has set us free. But we are *not* free, Lord, because we accept only the crown and not the cross. We love you, but not enough to risk the wrath of the powers that be. We love you, but not enough to take actions that will offend our friends. We love you, but not enough to make us love our enemies. We love you only enough to follow you where paths are smooth and well-trodden, not where few have dared to go. Forgive us, Lord, for the smallness of our love. Fill us with Christmas love so that our love, like yours, may reach out to the ends of the earth. Amen

74

Eternal God, we sing "Love Came Down at Christmas," and we thrill to the story of the infant Christ in the manger in Bethlehem, and to the promise of peace on earth to the people of good will. But we are not a people of good will. We harbor resentment in our lives because of real or imagined slights. We are envious of people who have more spiritual blessings than we do, and we treat despitefully those among us who are poor and powerless. Forgive us, Lord. Cleanse our hearts with your redeeming love so we may come to know the peace of Christmas within our lives, and so that we might become fit instruments in your hands for spreading that peace throughout every land. Amen

75

Eternal God, we fail to realize the promise of Christmas peace because we refuse to share anything we have, especially peace, with others. It does not bother us that peace is but a dream for others if *we* have peace. It does not bother us that many people are unloved, if *we* have a loving family, or loving friends. Forgive us our narrow self-concern, Lord. Help us to see we cannot know *real* peace until we do our best to see that others have it too. Amen

Prayers of Confession

76

O God, you hava given us so much. In this Advent season, we celebrate Christ's presence in our lives and prepare our hearts for your coming. Overlook our frailties, which so often blind us to your presence and to one another's needs. Forgive us when we live selfish little lives with little time for the needs of your children. Grant us the wisdom to see Christmas with the eyes of children, with awe and gratitude, so that our lives may take on a glow that will light up the lives of everyone we meet and so that we may be worthy of fellowship with you, the universal God, whose name is love. Amen

77

What must you think of us, Lord? So quickly the joy of Christmas leaves our lives. Christ came to free us from the fussiness and hypocrisy of Pharisaic religion, but very quickly the church began to create more and more rules for Christians to follow. For our part, we often put more emphasis on those rules than we do on our relationships with one another. Forgive us, Lord, for our failure to live loving and forgiving lives. Show us how we may make Christmas a part of our everyday lives so that we may spread joy throughout the world. May we learn not to take ourselves so seriously that we make Christianity a burden to be borne rather than an uplifting joy. Amen

78

You have given your Holy Spirit to all of us, Lord, and you have challenged us to receive this great gift with joy and with a heart prepared to take up its task. We start out with such good intentions, but obstacles wear down our good resolve. We become confused and turn to our leaders with a demand not for help in clarifying our thoughts but for easy answers. Forgive us, Lord, when we try to escape our responsibility by shifting it to our leaders. Give us the courage to live our lives out of the awareness that we are your children. May we never disgrace your holy name. Amen

79

Eternal God, we thank you for your love. The Bible tells us of your love for all your creation. Your prophets have told us of your glory, and how you desire for all your children to live in peace. You sent Christ, the great peacemaker, to show us the kind of love that can create the peace you desire for us. However, in our response to him, we try to make him over into our image. We have created "Christs" of every color and nationality. While it is important for us to realize that you care for each of us personally, such creations easily become monstrous distortions that cause us to shut other people out, to limit your love to us and to those who live and think like us. Forgive us, Lord. Help us to see that only as everyone is included in your love, and ours, can we have the peace we so desire. Amen

80

We come, O Lord, seeking wisdom and understanding, so that we may guide our footsteps wisely and somehow make sense of our world. We know that you promise good to us, but so much happens to us, or to friends, that seems only bad. Why, Lord? Is it something we have done, or is it a failure of our vision? Are we perhaps looking for the wrong thing, or in the wrong direction? Inform our hearts with your living Spirit, O Lord, so that we may find your peace in the midst of the warfare of this world. Amen

81

We thank you, Lord, for the love we know is ours in Christ, a love that offers peace. Quarrels divide us, and pride refuses to allow us to submit to any discipline that might enable us to work together. In the name of freedom, we create a chaos

Prayers of Confession

that undermines the creation of your kingdom. Forgive us, Lord. Teach us that, only as we submit to the bonds of love and seek to work in harmony with all your children, can we hope to know your peace which passes understanding. Amen

82

Eternal God, we hear your word of salvation, and we gladly respond. We are willing to lay down our lives for you, when necessity demands it. However, we are reasonable people, and "reasonable" people do not rock boats or cause unnecessary conflict. What we really mean is that we are more concerned with propriety than with justice, with keeping order than with doing what is right in a situation. We want to follow you, but we are unwilling to inconvenience ourselves or our friends, and so we tolerate blatant injustices, saying and doing only enough to quiet our consciences. Forgive us, Lord, our pettiness and our feeble attempts to serve you. Give us the courage to take a stand for righteousness, regardless of the personal cost so that we may be found worthy of you and deserving of your grace. Amen

83

You call us to follow you, Lord, and we are quite willing to do so, as long as you lead us through green pastures and beside still waters. However, it is another matter when you lead us through fields covered with thorns, over rugged mountains, or across raging rivers. Then, our courage fails us, and we hold back, thinking to wait for just a little, until things calm down. We assure ourselves that there is no hurry. After all, a thousand years is as a day in your sight. Forgive us, Lord. Help us to realize that *now* is the day of salvation. *Today* is the day we are to follow you. May no distance be too far and no path too steep for us to answer your call. Amen

84

Why is it, Lord, that we are so long on promises and so short on performance? The Bible warns us not to make promises unless we have every intention of carrying through. We *do* intend to, Lord. It's just that we get so busy that we forget. Slow us down, Lord, and help us sort out our priorities so that we remember to give you first place in our lives. Amen

85

O Lord, it costs so little to be kind, and yet even that little cost seems to be too much to us. We are either too busy or too self-concerned to notice the needy at our door. We dream of great things that we will do for you, yet we fail to see you when you come to us in the person of our neighbor, for whom we never seem to have time. "No time now," we say. "Come back when I'm not so busy." "No time now. I have to pray." "No time now. I must be off to church; I have a field to plow; etc." What must you think of our lack of vision and our lack of compassion, Lord? Forgive us, and break the cycle of our busyness so that we can stop long enough to see the opportunities for serving you that lie before us. Amen

86

Eternal God, you came to your people in Abraham and Moses, calling them to move beyond known borders, to trust in your guiding hand rather than in their traditions. You came to your people in Christ, calling them to lay aside cherished traditions they had received from Abraham and Moses, and to trust in you. Now, you are calling to us, and we, like those who have gone before us, are slow to answer. We place too much confidence in our ancestors and their traditions, and in doctrines created by human minds. We are so committed to them that we fail to realize that all doctrines and traditions are but poor attempts to grasp the mystery of your presence. Forgive us, Lord, and teach us to give our complete trust only to you, testing every tradition and every doctrine, new or old, as we seek to grow in our awareness of who you are and what you ask of us. Amen

Part 3

Prayers of Celebration

Prayers of Celebration

1

We thank you, Lord, for the promise of Christmas. Who does not get a warm feeling within, when they contemplate the infant Christ in the manger of Bethlehem? Such love as we find there is beyond our understanding. How could you love us so much that you would send your Son to redeem us, we who have so often proven unworthy of that love? Even now, our response is less than it should be, but your love does not waver. We are safely in your loving care, and nothing that the world can do can change that. Thank you, Lord, for such a love. We pray that your love will overflow in our hearts so that everyone we meet may experience the love that is Christmas. Amen

2

O Lord, we thank you for the Christmas story. It touches the hurting spots in our lives and soothes our troubled spirits. This world has need of Christmas. So many suffer want; so many are fearful; so many strike out in anger because of the hurts deep within their souls. Shed your Christmas love deep into their hearts, Lord. Use us as instruments of your love. Set our souls afire with a zeal for peace and love, and send us out into this dark world of ours with a message that will bring peace, hope, and love into the hearts of all people everywhere. Amen

3

O Lord, Christmas is a time for simple love that refuses to see the barriers that people erect in their hearts and their lives. Christ refused to see the barriers raised by the Pharisees which shut so many people out from the temple. Paul refused to see the barriers preventing women from being ministers, nor would he see the barriers separating Jews and Gentiles. May we, too, Lord, be filled with the simple love of Christmas, so that our love will extend to all people, and not just to people who see everything the way that we do. Amen

Prayers of Celebration

4

With joyful hearts, O Lord, we give you thanks for Christmas. The birth of Christ is a beacon light that guides our lives, no matter how dark our night. With Christ as guide, we are no longer afraid to live our lives in the open, where people can see us. Our dreams of peace seem not so far away when we see our future through the eyes of Christ. He gives us hope to go on when things seem darkest, but, most important, he teaches us to view one another with eyes of love so that we are able to create harmony where disunity and distrust would otherwise be. Grant us the grace of Christmas so that our lives may be a beacon light to our brothers and sisters, who still live in darkness, so that they, too, may come to know the peace and joy of Christmas. Amen

5

It's Christmas time again, Lord, the time when we celebrate your greatest gift to us: Christ. We enjoy the majesty of the mountains, the quiet beauty of the forest, and the raucous rambling of a mountain stream, all gifts from your generous hand, but none of the countless gifts we have received are like the gift of Christmas. Here, your love invades our lives, and we are regenerated so that we can take up our lives in the coming year, ever mindful that we are not alone. We walk through the darkest night unafraid, because of Christmas. We are able to see the good in others, even our worst enemies, because of Christmas. Guide us, Lord, as we try to live Christmas lives and as we try to open up the lives of those around us to this miracle we call Christmas. Amen

6

It's a new year, Lord, a time of endings, but also a time of beginnings. We have made many mistakes, but you bring to us the blessing of new beginnings. Not only are we given a new year, but we are also offered a new "world," *if* we really want it, with all our heart and soul. You will not force yourself on us, Lord, but you never abandon us to our own devices. You are ever near, calling us to new life. Bless us in this hour, Lord, so that our hearts may be open to the message of Christmas, and our lives might be enriched by the love which flows from your presence. Amen

7

Eternal God, it is hard for us to comprehend fully the Easter event. We know how undeserving we are of such love. It thrills our hearts to know that you care so much for us that you will not let us go. Each day is a brand new day, filled with possibilities for abundant life, because of your love for us. May we always be aware of the tremendous price Christ paid to awaken us to your love. In loving gratitude for such love we offer ourselves as a living sacrifice to your kingdom so that others may come to experience the Easter event in their lives. Amen

8

We thank you, God, for lives set free from dark despair, for lives redeemed from the dungeon of blind bigotry. We know that we are not all that we could be, but today we celebrate all that we are. You have made us. You have given us great gifts, and by these gifts we are enabled to escape the destructive lusts of this world, to share in your divine nature, and to become participants in the creation of your kingdom on earth. We hereby dedicate ourselves, our time, and our gifts to building up rather than tearing down, to growth rather than decay, and to the pursuit of love rather than hate. Amen

9

We thank you, God, for such a beacon light as Jesus to follow in our search for new and meaningful life, filled with real

Prayers of Celebration

relationahips. We gladly take up the lives that you offer us knowing that, though your way often leads to a cross, it is the only path to real life, joy and love. Guide us as we seek with sometimes blinded eyes for the way that you would lead us. Enrich our community so that we may be one in the Spirit and one in the Lord. Enable us to see clearly one another's needs so that we may be a ministering community. Forgive us when temptations lead us astray. Fill our lives with an awareness that Easter has taken place in our lives, creating in us a new way and a new day. Amen

10

For the love of mothers, Lord, we give you special thanks this day. No other love reminds us so much of your love. Often, we do not deserve our mother's love, but it is always there, ready to minister to our bumps and bruises and to kiss away our pains. Who but our mothers are so quick to forget the pain that we have caused them, or to appreciate a gift as ridiculous as dandelions? May we prove worthy of our mothers' love, Lord, living lives that would make them proud of us, and may we also prove worthy of your love, living lives that will gladden your heart. Amen

11

Within our families, Lord, we come to know something of your love. People come to know you apart from families, but there is nothing quite like a loving father and mother to awaken in us the first stirrings of love. Help us, Lord, as we strive to make our families even more a haven of love, treasuring our moments together, encouraging one another in our spiritual growth. May we use our families as a launching pad into life, not an escape from life, and may we never forget the lessons of love we have learned within the sanctuary of our families. Amen

12

For all the joys of Spring we thank you, God. For food to eat and water to drink, we are humbly grateful. You have created such a beautiful world and given us such an important part in preserving it. When we look at the mountains that tower above us, and at the fields that lie around us, our hearts are filled with thanks. Enable us, by your continuing presence, to be good stewards of all you have given us so that our children and our children's children may also thrill to the glory of Spring and your abiding love. Amen

13

We celebrate today, Lord, your gift of the Holy Spirit. As the disciples of Jesus received the Holy Spirit long ago, and found in that presence the strength to face all manners of persecution, and even death, so too we may receive your Holy Spirit into our lives this Pentecost, if we but open our hearts. In the power of the Holy Spirit, we can take up our lives and live them triumphantly, even if the whole world should turn against us. With the Holy Spirit as our guide, there is no enemy we need fear, no situation we cannot face with courage and hope. We take up our lives, Lord, and live them in your name, knowing that your Holy Spirit will give us the strength to carry out our resolve. Amen

14

Thank you, Lord, for Pentecost. Today we celebrate the gift of your Holy Spirit to Jesus' disciples, a gift that changed them from cowards, hiding themselves away, into courageous messengers of your Gospel of love. They left their places of hiding and travelled throughout the world to bring the light of your Gospel to people trapped in pagan darkness. May we, like them, receive your Holy Spirit, so that we may leave *our* hiding places and proclaim openly your message of hope and love, for our world is also a world filled with pagan darkness, in need of the light which only you can give. Amen

Prayers of Celebration

15

We hear, Lord God, your promise of a transformed life, and we thrill at the thought of being a new community in Christ. You have given us so many and varied gifts, gifts that have the power to transform our lives and the lives of everyone in the world who will listen to you. Open our hearts, Lord, that we may truly listen. Give us courage so that we may stand strong in the hours of trial that are sure to come when your Word conflicts with the voice of this world, with its love for glory and power. And help us, Lord, to withstand the temptation, so strong in all of us, as it was in Peter, to seek for power and glory. Teach us that it is in service, even suffering service, that we fulfill our calling in Christ. Amen

16

Eternal God, our great and gracious redeemer, your love explodes in our hearts with a power that is breath-taking. Tasks that seemed beyond our capabilities are performed with ease, and obstacles that once would have stopped us in our tracks are barely able to make us pause. Your presence enables us to forget that pride which often separates us from certain people so that we are able to involve ourselves in their lives with such love that their opposition (and ours) just melts away. Armed with your love, we indeed find that the roughest places are made plain, and we are able to walk in newness of life. We walk with sunlight in our lives because our lives are grounded in your love, touched by the fire of Christ's love and fulfilled in our union with our neighbor. May all people praise you and find your presence in their lives. Amen

17

Lord, our lives have known despair, but that was only when we lost the way and set upon unchartered seas without the benefit of your guiding Spirit. When at last our pride was broken, and we regained our senses and returned to you, we found the power to turn our lives around. Problems that once loomed so large seem as nothing within the presence of your Holy Spirit. Thank you, Lord, for never giving up on us, even when we are intent on giving up on you. Thank you for your Son, who gave us such a fine example to follow, who told us of a love that would never let us go. Amen

18

We are thankful, Lord, for your presence. You lift us when we are weary. Your presence brings calm to our untranquil days. Our fears subside, and our hearts are filled with your peace. We are enabled to pick up the pieces of our daily lives and to carry on. Teach us to pray so that we may hear your Word for our lives. Give us courage so that, hearing, we may obey, counting not the cost of our decision but only the inward joy that awaits those who choose to follow you. Amen

19

Almighty God, your people of all the ages live and praise you. In our communion with you, we have communion with generations past and generations yet unborn. Before your throne we are one with a great multitude, which no one could number, and in praising you we join with people from every nation. As we celebrate communion and accept your offer of a new covenant, may we come to a better understanding of our relationship with you and with one another, so that we may truly be a healing and redeeming community. Amen

Part 4

General Prayers

1

We come, O Lord, with chastened hearts
for we have strayed away
from paths that you would call us to.
So often when we pray
we ask you to remove from us
the burdens that we bear,
not knowing they were meant to help
us show how much we care
for those less fortunate than us.
Guide us, Lord, so we
may see the burdens that we have
were meant to set us free.

2

This day, and every day, O Lord,
we need your presence near,
to fill our minds with thoughts of love
that leave no room for fear.
Fill our hearts with gentle love
that does not cease to care
for people whose actions seem designed
to drive us to despair.
For only thus can we become
true followers of your Son,
who taught us that a loving heart
will never come undone.

3

Speak to our hearts and lead us, Lord,
lest we should stumble in the way
your Holy Spirit directs our lives.
You know our feet are made of clay,
and we do not desire a cross.

General Prayers

Indeed, we are quick to count the cost
and turn away if it's too high.
Lest we be numbered with the lost,
inspire our hearts to follow Christ
as instruments of righteousness,
so that our lives may bring to all
a sense of joy and blessedness.

4

O God, who holds us in his hands,
help us bring peace to all the lands.
Enable us to be alive
to truth and love. So may we strive
for purity that sees your light
shining in the darkest night.
So may we be a holy band
of followers, who never stand
for cruelty, who never seek
for gain that harms the poor or weak.
Help us be forever true,
content to live our lives for you

5

Teach us to be open, Lord,
to life and love and you,
so that our lives may be as fresh
as early morning dew.
Ease the pain within our hearts
and grant that peace of mind
which comes from resting in your love
and serving all mankind.
Grant that we may ever find
that deep tranquility
where love and joy and peace abide
in true community.
Teach each one to bless your name

with deep humility
that vaunts not self but rests content
within humanity.

6

In loving trust,
we turn to you, O God.
We know, that in your love,
our lives can grow
until we reach the stars.
Enable us to also love
with patient friendliness,
that disarms hate
and makes peace a reality.

7

Eternal God, our dwelling place
for untold ages, renew
our hearts and minds so that our lives
may become an avenue
of faith, that travelers stranded here
with hope replaced by fear,
may follow, and in following may find
that fear will disappear,
if only they will trust your love.
Restore our faith today
so that we might be used by you
in showing others your way.

8

We turn, O Lord, to your command,
accepting all you give.
Forgive us when we close our eyes,
forgetting how to live
in fellowship and loving trust.

General Prayers

We are so quick to lie
when faced with failure's fruit.
Hear our anguished cry
as we turn back for comfort now.
Do not hold back your grace,
but hold us fast within your love
which can all our sins erase.

9

Your presence fills our cup, O Lord,
and we are filled indeed,
when through your Holy Spirit you come
to us in our hour of need.
No one is unimportant to you.
The least of us is just
as great as a king upon his throne.
You teach us how to trust
in life again, and so we sing
our praise to your holy name
and promise never more to cause
you to look away in shame
because of something we have done.
In ever constant prayer
we'll demonstrate unto the world
how much we really care.

10

Our Lord and our God, you know our shame —
how we have sinned against your name.
So often it seems, to our regret,
we turn to you and say, "Not yet!"
We did not mean to go astray —
we only wished a small delay.
Forgive us, Lord, and as we pray,
please lead us in your righteous way.

11

We give you thanks, O Lord, because your peace
informs our hearts and leads us homeward through
the murk and mire that threatened to increase
beyond our powers to conquer or subdue.
Our dark night gives way to blessed tranquility
because our lives have found their source at last.
When we passed through our Garden of Gethsemane,
and cast our lot with you, the sins of our past
released their hold, and life became once more
a song to sing, no longer a cross to bear,
and on the wind of your Spirit, our souls now soar
beyond the triviality of despair.
We give our lives to you, content to know
your Holy Spirit will keep our lives aglow.

12

We stand in awe before you, Lord,
and seek your will,
so that our lives may come to be
more Christlike.
We freely own our vanity
and seek your love,
forgiving and kind,
that freshens as the winds
that blow away the smog
from hearts long slaves of fear.

13

We celebrate your love, O Lord,
your love and tenderness,
which promises more to us than all
the trinkets we possess,
for love makes life well worth the living
and feeds our starving soul,

General Prayers

and takes up lives the world has broken
and makes them once more whole.
Touch us with your Holy Spirit
so we may be alive
to ways to create an atmosphere
in which everyone can thrive.

14

O God, preserver of our life,
your presence fills our heart,
and we find strength to live each day.
No longer living apart
from you, we find our strength renewed,
and problems that once brought fear,
within the light of godly fear,
are quick to disappear.
Invade our hearts and bring your peace
so we may ever dare
to be perceived by all the world
as those who truly care.

15

Your will, O Lord, is plain, if we would see
beyond the narrow confines of our zeal
and listen to the Christ of Galilee.
His presence in our hearts would soon reveal
to us the healing Word that does not end
at boundary lines religion loves to set.
We find in Christ the everlasting friend
whose promise is that he will not forget
us when all other friends have turned away.
He gives to us the task of proclaiming peace
to all who prepare their hearts for judgment day
and set their minds and hearts on love's increase.
We find your will when we forget our own
and build our lives on Christ, the cornerstone.

16

Come, O Lord, within our heart.
Create, therein, a place apart
from our busy world so we may hear
your healing Word that casts out fear.
Encourage us to reach a hand
to everyone within our land,
so we may all, with one accord,
live according to your Word
in unity that never ends,
that changes enemies to friends.

17

Inspire our hearts to love and praise,
to noble gentleness,
that will not harm a broken heart,
but only seeks to bless.
Too often, in our zeal, O Lord,
we use your holy name
to punish those who won't conform,
to point a finger of shame.
Forgive us such bad piety
and guide us in the way
that will create a better world,
beginning with today.

18

Speak, Lord, in the quiet of this hour,
and still our busyness
so we may turn our thoughts to you,
forgetting sweet success.
May nothing come between the love
that binds us to your way;
may nothing take so much of our time
that we forget to pray.

General Prayers

Your holy kingdom we adore
and pledge our loyalty.
We gladly serve and give ourselves
with all humility.

19

We bless you, Lord, for being there
when we had need of you,
for lifting up our tired heads
and showing us a view
that strengthened and supported hope
in a world made bright and new.
Supported by your presence here,
we promise to be true
to every task you lay before us.
With hopeful hearts we pursue
that love which neither death nor fear
have any power to subdue.

20

Sweeten up our lives, O Lord,
that we may know the joy
that nothing in this crazy world
can tarnish or destroy.
Unleash the love that lies within
so we may create a life
that plants a rose whose heavenly scent
can soothe away our strife.
Teach us to use our gifts in ways
that build community,
and put an end to every form
of subtle slavery.

21

Your gracious presence fills our hearts,

O Lord, and all our fear
just melts away. Your gracious love
creates an atmosphere
that renders possible what once
was but a foolish dream:
a great community that grants
to each his self-esteem.
And in this hope we find at last
the courage to seek a way
to create within our wilderness
a glimpse of the King's Highway.

22

O Lord, in all humility
we seek your loving grace
that is so freely given to all
who truly seek your face.
So long we've sought for foolish things,
things to give us pride.
Now we only ask that your love
may in our hearts abide.
Too long we've followed in the way
that leads to ecstasy.
Now we take our cross and go
to dark Gethsemane.

23

When we are weighed in the balance, Lord,
just where will we be found?
Will we find our lives are on the rock
or just on sandy ground?
Will we be sorry for our past
or be, with justice, proud
that we have served our blessed Lord
and not the lonely crowd?
Have mercy on us when you judge

General Prayers

whatever we have been
and help us turn from tempting ways
that only lead to sin.

24

We thank you, God, for seasons past,
when you were there to guide
those, brave of soul, who dared to seek
your face, who would not hide
in platitudes that could not hope
to ever satisfy
the unrest that lay deep inside.
May we, like them, defy
the dim unknown to seek your face,
so we may find that grace
that has the power to release us from
the trite and commonplace.

25

Thank you, Lord, for being there
within our hour of need,
forgiving us when we were lost
because of wanton greed.
May we, like you, reach out in love
to others who are lost,
telling them of Christ's great love,
that comes without any cost,
a love that sets us free to grow
to our fullest ability
and promises joy to those who try
to set their brother free.

26

We thank you, God, that you have seen
our need for holiness.

It is so easy to lose your love
when we forget to bless
the lives of those who come our way.
Be with us in this hour
as we seek to open our hearts and minds
so we may receive the power
of your Holy Spirit within our lives.
Then we will clearly see
that holiness and reverence
are part of our destiny.

27

In quiet trust we will prepare
for times when blessings seem so far
away. We know how much you care,
and so we'll follow after the star
of David, no matter how dim it seems.
We'll leave our lives within your hand
and work to fashion better dreams
for those who follow your command
to take their cross and lead the way
for those whose souls are still unfree.
Help us, Lord, as now we pray
for wisdom to see our destiny.

28

Within your presence, Lord,
we hear your living Word,
and we can then become
what you would have us be.
Your love redeems our life
and banishes all strife,
and when we follow you,
our souls at last are free.
Be with us in this hour,
and by your loving power

open up our eyes
so we may truly see.

29

Our blessed Lord, your glory shines
within the darkest place,
and even those with dimmest faith
perceive your gentle grace.
Help us, like those who went before
to show the holy way,
be guides to those whose lives are now
in shattered disarray,
so they may find the hope they seek.
Forgive us when we try
to limit you to our design
so we can gratify
our desire for certainty. Grant us
the wisdom somehow to grow
beyond the petty boundaries
of the little that we know.

30

With joy we come before our God
whose love will never end.
He sees beyond the selfishness
to which we often tend.
Forgive us, Lord, and lift our hearts
above our selfish ways,
and may our voices and our lives
forever sing your praise.

31

Come to us, Lord, lest we forget
the way before us that you have set
when things seem out of our control.

When trials test our very soul,
we trust in you to be our guide.
Though storms press in on every side,
your Spirit soothes our soul within,
preserving us from foolish sin
and warning of the grievous harm
that lurks beneath its outward charm.
Give courage to our fainting heart,
so we may dare to do our part
to create within this hungry land
a desire to follow your command.

32

Be present, Lord, throughout our land,
and teach us all that you command,
of those who seek to find the life
that you have promised, where the strife
that fills our world can never reach.
Give us the courage, too, to teach
the people that we meet that there
is hope and joy beyond compare
awaiting those who fill their hearts
with the love your Holy Spirit imparts.

33

May we bring your kingdom closer, Lord,
to all who live in fear,
teaching them how the love of Christ
can make it disappear,
and may we serve in humility,
controlling that foolish pride
that makes us close our hearts to those
we think unsanctified.
In wisdom and true godliness,
we'll count ourselves content
to be of service to our land,

General Prayers

as those whom Christ has sent
to bring his peace where fear now reigns.
They are content indeed
who serve you, Lord, not just with words
but by serving those in need.

34

We find a vision, Lord,
when we trust in you,
and life takes on more meaning
whenever we are true
to all that you have called us.
Grant us in this hour
the courage to be true,
the will to trust your power
in everything we do.

35

Be present in our lives, O Lord;
forgive our foolish ways.
So blinded by the light of day
we forget to sing your praise.
So many hearts are famished, Lord,
for news to set them free;
so many eyes are blinded, Lord,
and cannot even see
that love that is so freely given
to everyone in need.
Enable us to spread the word
that Christ is Lord indeed.

36

Eternal God, our dwelling place
for untold ages, renew
our hearts and minds so that our lives

may become an avenue
of faith, that travelers stranded here,
with hope replaced by fear,
may follow, and, in following, may find
that fear will disappear
if only they will trust your love.
Restore our faith today
so that we might be used by you
in showing others your way.

37

O loving God, inform our hearts
so we may learn to be
alive to all the joy within
your world. No great decree
exists to tell us how to live,
but Christ has shown the way:
True life is found by those who strive
to usher in your day.
Enable us to live our lives
in quiet forgetfulness
that only has this one desire:
some other life to bless.

38

In loving memory, O Lord,
we come before you now
to seek your blessing in our lives.
As we renew our vow
to serve you in our land, forgive
our foolish little pride
that causes us to stand aside,
when we should stand "beside,"
all people in their needs. Inflame
our hearts with love, and lead
us in the paths of righteousness,
so that we may be yours indeed.

General Prayers

39

We follow, Lord, where Christ has gone,
so that our lives may bring the dawn
of your redeeming grace to those
enclosed in sin's dark night, who close
their hearts and minds to your saving Word
and blindly follow the world like a herd
of sheep. Enable us to bring
the light of love to those who cling
to outworn ways and do not dare
to even show how much they care.
May we, in love, show them the way
that leads to your eternal day.

40

O Lord of Love, please set me free
to be the person I ought to be.
My eyes are dim, my hearing dull.
My only hope is the miracle
of your sweet love that clears the heart
of disappointed dreams. Impart
your grace and open up my eyes
so I may come to realize,
within my life, the promise of joy
that little men cannot destroy,
a joy that comes from deep within
when you have freed us from our sin.

41

O God, evolver of my being,
fulfill your work in me.
Establish now your temple here
and set your people free,
free to become a special band
intent on your command,

quick to stand for what we believe
in this and every land.
With our lips and our lives, may we commend
ourselves to you this day,
and may we spread to all the world
the news of the living way.

42

O God, empowerer of our lives,
our future is in your hands,
and yet, so often your love is spurned
in many different lands.
The past is too much with us, Lord;
we hold it close with fear,
refusing to be satisfied
just to have you near.
Encourage us to cast aside
our foolishness and pride,
so that your love, within our hearts,
may evermore abide.

43

O God, your presence drives out fear
and fills our life with song.
Empower us to sing your praise
and end the night of wrong.
When we are wont to wring our hands,
despairing of your grace,
awaken love and peace within
our hearts, and remove every trace
of sadness there. Within your love
we find escape from despair,
and the only price of admission there
is simple, heartfelt prayer.

General Prayers

44

The world is ever present, Lord;
it thunders in our ear;
it seeks to lead us from your will
through enticement and through fear.
O let your still, small voice
pierce the armor of our vanity;
O may your soft and gentle love
set every one of us truly free.
Proclaim your Word to us
in the stillness of this hour.
Come into our hearts and minds
with all your majesty and power.

45

Be present, Lord, and guide our steps
along our inward way,
for only when we follow you
are we children of the day.
Our lives are so possessed by fear
that only you can set us free
and open up our hearts and eyes,
so that we clearly see
the path that even now before
us lies, a path made dim
when we are tossed about like leaves
before our every whim.
Grant us the courage to persevere
in following the way
that Christ prepared for those who dare
to start anew each day.

46

In loving trust,
we turn to you, O God.

We know, that in your love,
our lives can grow
until we reach the stars.
Enable us to also love
with patient friendliness
that disarms hate
and makes peace a reality.

47

To love, to live
each moment now
that God does give —
were my whole life
to justice given
despite the strife —
then would I see
such bliss that comes
to souls set free.
To be so near,
and yet so far,
because of fear —
why must we turn
away from God
for whom we yearn?
Only in you
may we find love
forever free.
Grant us your peace
so that our flight
from fear may cease
and we may find
secure abode
within your mind.

General Prayers

48

God of the universe, source of our souls
our lives find their meaning
when we give ourselves to you.
Teach us to rest secure
within your truthfulness,
so that we may make our land
a place of blessedness.

49

The Lord is here
for those with eyes to see,
and so we turn our hearts
to sounds that silently
address our world.
Speak softly, Lord,
and we will listen now.

50

We seek, O Lord, for foolish things,
not knowing what your love can bring.
We seek for peace and self-control,
and find we've lost our very soul.
We aim too low, and thus we lose
the very life that we would choose,
if we but knew the price we pay
for living only for today.
Open our eyes so we may see
that when we love we're truly free.

51

Our eyes are dim, our hearing lost,
but still your voice cuts through the ice
within our veins
and warms our tired and thoughtless brains.
Release us, Lord, from gilded chains,
self-imposed by thoughtless words

and angry deeds.
Warm up our hearts until our eyes
perceive the love that has the power
to set us free.

52

You call us, Lord,
to find a dream beyond our own horizons,
but we, in fear, forget the task
and seek our visions in a glass.
You create our world anew,
and call to us with shouts of gladness;
you offer us the greatest joy,
of lives enriched with purpose,
but we instead choose silent death
and walk as those before a grave,
who whisper lest the dead have ears.
Forgive our selfish sanctimony,
excuses reeking innocent blood,
and teach us how to open doors
to life forever new.

53

Eternal God, O God of truth,
how fearsome is your gaze,
for we have left the path of truth
for worldly wisdom's ways.
Hold back your wrath, though well deserved,
and love us once again.
Perhaps your love may lure us back
to calmer days, and then,
when at last our senses have returned,
and once more we sing your praise,
the light of your eternal love
will guide our nights and days.
So guide our steps in the days to come,

as you did within our youth,
and we will pledge to live our lives
according to your truth.

54

Hear us, Lord, as we pray;
teach us so to live each day
that we may find your guiding light
even in our darkest night.
Nothing do we need to fear
knowing you are ever near.
Gladly will we face each day
knowing that you lead the way.

55

There are so many people, Lord,
without a chance to be
the way that you intended them —
a people truly free.
The bonds they wear are ours, O Lord,
though fashioned without care;
we simply did not stop to think
of whether it was fair.
We walk in absentmindedness
amidst great loneliness,
and do not see that we could bring
your peace and blessedness.
Give us the eyes to see, O Lord,
the loneliness and greed,
so that our lives at last may serve
to answer deep-felt needs.

56

You called us, Lord, so here we are.
Enable us to see your star

within the wilderness of a life
devoted to foolishness and strife.
Prepare us for your blessed truth.
Encourage old, and also youth,
to accept the pain of being new,
to take up their cross and follow you.

57

O God, protector of our past,
be present with us here,
as we attempt to move beyond
our fences and our fear.
Teach us how to accept these days
and everything they bring,
so even in our darkest days
we don't forget to sing
your praise for all that you have done
to ease our bed of pain.
Protect us from that foolish pride
which makes all living vain
and lead us in your living way
of love and joyful praise,
till we have learned to live our lives
in consecrated ways.

58

We heed, O Lord, your call to come
and seek you in this place.
We gladly hear your clarion call
which nothing can erase.
We lay our lives upon your altar,
not asking for the light
we need to see our way, but trusting
that you will lead us right.
Shed forth your light within our hearts
so we may see within

General Prayers

and know ourselves for what we are,
and what we might have been.
Help us to follow in the way
that leads to truth and light,
content to work for nothing less
than what we believe is right.

59

We serve God unawares
or serve him not at all,
for when we seek salvation
our hearts can't hear his call.
Our God does not desire
to set our souls on fire
with zeal for our own soul,
but for the world entire.
If we would serve our God,
our lives we must repent,
for almost all our time
on thoughts of self are spent.
O teach us in this hour
to know your will and way,
lest we should count the cost
of serving you each day.

60

Forgive us, Lord, when we remain
where peace and quiet lie,
while all around this weary world
oppressed and needy cry
for help against the dark despair
they face on every side.
Grant us the courage, Lord, to let
the Holy Spirit guide
our lives in paths where fiery storms
may seem to bar the way,

General Prayers

so we may show to everyone
the promise of Christmas-day.

61

We thank you, Lord, for days of joy
that set our spirits free,
for Christ who taught us of the worth
of true humility,
for those who have the simple grace
to serve humanity
and yet not feel the need to rule
with petty tyranny.
May Christmas be to us a time
of joyful victory,
when we can celebrate your love
in peace and harmony.

62

We give our lives
that we may be,
secure within
your love, set free.
Enable us
to show your love
to those with lives
devoid of love,
so they may know
your tender care
through that concern
with which we share.
We give our lives
because we know
we receive them back
with a special glow,
for joy abides
within the heart

General Prayers

wherein your love
plays a vital part.

63

We are yours, O God,
and gladness fills our heart
to know that you chose
us to play a mighty part
within your plan for us.
Teach us, Lord, to seek
your living presence here
in everything we do,
letting neither peace nor fear
destroy our love for you.

64

Forgive us, Lord, whenever we set
upon the vengeance road,
and open our eyes so we may see
our brothers' heavy load
of sin and sorrow. Open up
our hearts so we may feel
the pain that turns their love to hate.
Encourage us to lay
aside opinions quickly formed,
so we may carefully weigh
the reasons people act so cruel
to those they do not know.
Inspire us to meet their hate
with love, so we may show
to them the living way of Christ,
for only love's increase
can turn aside a person's hate
and give him inner peace.

65

Come, O Lord, within our heart.
Create therein a place apart
from our busy world, so we may hear
your healing Word that casts out fear.
Encourage us to reach a hand
to everyone within our land,
so we may all, with one accord,
live according to your Word
in unity that never ends,
that changes enemies to friends.

66

We come, Lord,
alone, but not quite alone,
aware, but not quite aware.
Our fields of vision
are too close and cramped.
We have not learned from Christ
the art of open hearts.
Enlarge our hearts,
and then our souls
will chart the universe
and beg for more.

67

Forgive us, Lord, when we forget
our responsibility
to reach out with the hand of love
to those who are not free.
When we are hurt, remind us, Lord,
of dark Gethsemane,
where Christ so freely chose the cross
to serve humanity
which often scorned his loving ways.

Like him, may we reach out
in love to those who scorn our love,
who only think to shout
obscenities in answer to
our words of quiet peace.
May we continue in your love
till all quarrels and wars shall cease.

68

Christ speaks, if we will only hear,
and turn away from sin,
but we, instead, make up a game
and pretend to follow him,
yet all the while it is so plain
that we have made the rules,
such rules designed to hide the fact
that we have played the fool.
God calls us to return to him
before it is too late,
and we are left so all alone
outside the heavenly gate.
Though we are blind and will not see,
he does not turn away,
but ever seeks to bring us back
unto his holy way.

69

Lord, grant us faith that we may be
your people for eternity.
Forgive us when we go astray
from Christ who is the living way,
whose love was given without cost
to those whose lives seemed almost lost.
Like him, may we be messengers
of peace, till everyone concurs
that Christmas is for everyone

and all bow down before the Son,
and gladly give up everything,
finding in him the signet ring
that promises eternity
and sets our troubled spirits free.

70

Your love becomes a light, O Lord,
that brightens up our days,
and that is why we come to you
and gladly sing your praise.
May we become, in turn, a source
of joy to everyone
we meet, so they may come to know
that you provide the sun
to warm their days. In love we go
to places others fear,
to tell to those with questing hearts
that Christ the Lord is here.

71

We are so tempted, Lord,
by things we can't control
that seldom do we have
a truly worthy goal.
Forgive those narrow thoughts
that often lead us astray,
and guide us back once more
into your holy way.
As you reached out to us,
may we reach out our hand,
till peace and love shall reign
throughout our lonely land.

General Prayers

72

We are so impatient, Lord.
We find it hard to keep
our spirits up when we see
things that make us weep.
Your Word falls on deaf ears,
and people go their way
not knowing of the love
you offer them today.
Revive our spirits, Lord,
and teach us, as we pray,
to let today's own troubles
be sufficient for the day.

73

We need your presence, Lord,
if we would do your will.
Forgive our foolish pride
and teach us to be still,
to listen to your voice
and wait upon your Word,
lest in our foolish pride
our lives become absurd.
Your presence brings us joy,
releasing in our lives
the power sin had trapped,
so that our hope revives.

74

We turn to you, O God,
cleansed of our deep despair,
for we are in your love
and know your gentle care.
We know that we are weak,
and prone to hesitate —

our fears and foolishness
often keep us fully awake.
We need your tender care
to lead us on our way,
and so we turn to you
upon this holy day.
Forget our foolish past,
forgive our selfishness,
and lead us ever more
into your blessedness.
May we become as one
in devotion to your name,
and may our lives reveal
your everlasting flame.
Our joy will know no bounds
so long as we remain
in true dependence on
your blessed, holy name.

75

Be gracious when we go astray,
and darkness marks our every day,
or days will ever seem too long,
and we may never hear your song.
Grant to us, within this hour,
the sense to feel your present power
within our lives. Then we will know
a joy that keeps our hearts aglow,
and we will find that every place
is filled with your redeeming grace.

76

Prepare us, Lord, to be with you,
to walk your way our whole life through.
Take from our lips the easy lie
that causes us to falsify

our righteousness. Be present, Lord,
as we begin to seek your Word
for us. Enable us to trust
in truth, to never be unjust
to anyone, so we may earn
that blessed peace for which we yearn.